Focused Investing:

Higher Returns With Lower Risk

Without Diversifying

Table of Contents

Preface
- *Who this book is for*
- *Why I wrote this book*
- *Who I am*

Introduction
- *Success and Focus*

I. Rebalancing and Diversification Are Keeping You Poor
- *Diversification vs. Focus*
- *Rebalancing*
- *Dollar Cost Averaging*
- *Mutual Funds and Advisers*
- *Mutual Funds and Dollar Cost Averaging*

II. Investing Like a Business
- *How Businesses Diversify*
- Chapter 1: Identify Potential Investments
  - *Economics and History*
  - *Top Down Approach*
  - *What Industry to Invest In*
  - *Penny Stocks*
  - *WalMart*
  - *Business Strategy*
  - *Five Forces Explained*
  - *The Fundamentals*
    - What to Buy
  - *Technical Tools*
    - When to Buy
    - Technical Signals
    - When to Sell

    Strategy From Start to Finish ....
  Chapter 2: Consider Risk and Return in Context..
  Chapter 3: Limit the Downside ....
    Risk and Return ....
    Types of Risk ....
    Options ....
        Buying Calls..
        Buying Puts...
    Stop Loss Technical Analysis..
    Protective Puts...

III. Develop Your Own Investing Style..
  Chapter 1: Consider What Not To Do...
  Chapter 2: Getting A Strategy ....
    Investment Strategy ....
    Developing Your Own Strategy ....
    Building Confidence ....
  Chapter 3: Start Focusing..
    BAII Plus ....

DISCLAIMER

INVESTMENTS INVOLVE RISK. LOSSES MAY OCCUR AT TIMES. THE ADVICE IN THIS BOOK IS TO BE TAKEN AT THE READER'S OWN DISCRETION. BY TAKING THE ADVICE CONTAINED THIS BOOK, THE READER AGREES TO RELEASE THE AUTHOR AND ANY RELATED PARTIES TO THE AUTHOR FROM ANY AND ALL LEGAL LIABILITY.

PREFACE

Who this book is for

This book is written for those that want to know more about investing and have the drive to do it on their own but may lack confidence. If this is you, this book will not only show you how to invest for yourself, it will give you the tools to reduce risk even if you only invest in one company. It will teach you how to pick low risk, high potential investments and then lower the risk further with technical signals and other tools. But most of all, it will help you stop procrastinating, gain experience, and build confidence - which spills over into other aspects of life. This book can be read at any skill level from beginning investors to experts. A word of caution: it takes money to make money. I am not talking about your investments themselves, I'm referring to the research costs and time. The research itself is minimal, yet many people neglect to do it. At a minimum you should subscribe to a few monthly investment magazines, it is a small cost that will pay off in the end.

Why I wrote this book

It is easier now than ever before in history to invest for yourself, even if you do not have much money. Yet there aren't many investment books that are easy to follow and give sound investment tips. Many books have attacked mutual funds for high fees and subpar performance but people still feel that they cannot invest successfully on their own. This is due to a lack of knowledge in some areas, as well as misinformation and myths instead of sound business advice. Because investing requires time, effort, knowledge, and research, many of these other books advocate shortcuts like investing in index funds. In my view, they are nearly as bad as mutual funds because of rebalancing (basically they don't buy and hold). Why this is bad will be explained. But I hope to help others gain confidence in their investing abilities. Confidence must come before success if it is to be lasting.

Who I am

Investing can be complicated and there are many books to read to help you with it. Why should you read mine? Aside from holding a masters degree in Financial Analysis I have tested multiple strategies and newsletters to determine for myself the best way to invest successfully. I have studied the best investors and most successful businesses, as well as the many failures. I will teach you to be confident in your own abilities. I will teach you not just how to get better returns, but at better odds (lower risk). The idea that you must take greater risk to get higher returns is only somewhat true and I will help you be one of the few who can invest for high return at low risk.

INTRODUCTION

This book is written for those who want to get ahead financially in life. It is very different from any other financial book you have probably read. This book is the culmination of knowledge from studying and observing success and wealth. The most successful people and companies find what they are good at, what they are interested in, and focus all their energy and time on becoming the best or most knowledgeable in that area. No business begins by being diversified! If it did it would fail. When most companies start to diversify they are seeking growth when their markets are saturated. They are not usually seeking to reduce risk. In fact, the most successful way for a company to diversify is to expand by using its core strengths, meaning they should avoid true diversification into entirely different and incompatible industries. So why should you do what businesses avoid doing? I wrote this book in order to help regular people invest for abnormal gains while achieving an understanding of risk and learning how to control it. Diversifying does nothing to control risk and only addresses one type of risk - market (or systematic) risk.

There are many myths and misconceptions about investing. You may have heard stories about the next big thing that is going to change the world; 3D printing and green technology come to mind, but there are many others. Some of these next big thing fads are things you have never heard of, which should be a huge warning sign. Don't ignore something new, but it is wise to do your own research. If financial data is hard to find or is not reported, that is another huge warning sign. The old saying, "Invest in what you know", does not mean invest in companies you are familiar with as much as it means find out about your investments. "Buy and Hold", does not mean buy and hope for the best. It should be revised instead to be: "Buy, Monitor, and Hold if conditions are satisfactory." "Buy low and sell high" does not really mean anything, it's just what everyone is trying to do. Some say, "Buy high and sell higher", which is just as useless. Warren Buffett says "Be greedy when others are fearful and fearful when others are greedy." I like this advice but I was also let down by it in the past (not because it is bad advice but because I was inexperienced in investing). I would like to put my own spin on that and revise it to "Be greedy *before* others are greedy and fearful *before* others are fearful." Another myth is that "What goes up must come down". While this is true for all things in the end, companies may continue to go up for decades before that fateful drop. You want the intrinsic value to grow with the stock, which just means cash flows, sales, and earnings are rising with the stock.

You may come to the conclusion after reading this book that it makes sense to invest in your education and skills, more so than the art of investing. While this is possible and this is what I have done, although I chose investing as my education, it may be too risky to rely on one set of skills your entire life. I have not studied only the stock market and investing strategies. I have studied history and economics as well. I worked in other fields giving me experiences and skills outside of investing. However, I do encourage progress in your field and in any field that interests you. I would not advocate studying anything that is not interesting to you, I suggest you find a link to something that is. If you are a doctor, you may have an advantage over other investors (the market) in that field, study medical companies and invest in them. I would also encourage finding an interest in something that is likely to have growing demand for a long time and to avoid gaining skills that will become obsolete.

Success and Focus

Napoleon Hill and John C. Maxwell are two examples of authors who have studied success and tell us that focusing on one purpose is a strong determinant of success. My purpose was to understand business, economics, and investments. Your purpose may be to create life saving drugs, music, or something else. So that means you should spend most of your time learning to be the best at what you do instead of putting all your time into studying investments as I have. This is ok because most of what you need to know can be learned in just a year through experience, reading, and staying current on issues. Finding great investments takes some research and can be time consuming, but you do not have to find the best investments in order to do well. You do not have to know how to use all of the tools in this book. There are other tools not mentioned in this book, that you may want to use. I have created a strategy based on observations of successful people and investments. The basic principle of this strategy is to always gain knowledge before investing. Do research and never rely on hype or marketing to make decisions, then take the most promising investments and limit losses. Do not sell the investment unless much better opportunities arise or the situation for the industry or company changes for the worse.

Napoleon Hill helped me to stop procrastinating and that is the number one reason most of us are not rich. Successful people do not worry and hope; they take action. The key is to find one thing you love and have a goal to become the best at it. That may be too ambitious for some, but it is a journey not a destination; meaning that you never get there, so as long as you try your best that is good enough. You will be getting better and that is what matters. Find something you love. As you gain knowledge or skills you feel better about yourself and this fuels a positive cycle to where you are getting better and better and it doesn't seem like effort, although it may be stressful at times. All successful people have one thing in common; they focus physically, mentally, and financially. They gain knowledge, do their own research, and make up their own minds. They consider others' viewpoints but they do not accept what others think as fact, without evidence.

I. REBALANCING AND DIVERSIFICATION ARE KEEPING YOU POOR

Diversification vs. Focus

I know, you have always been told to diversify. Look around your city, state, or country at all the richest people. They likely are invested in one business or one industry. This does not mean you should not diversify, but that you should do it with a strategy in mind. Mutual funds are usually overly diversified and have little or no strategy for wealth maximization, they only address risk minimization. When mutual funds do have a strategy it isn't very effective because of rules and constraints placed on the money. They may only be allowed to invest 1% of assets in one stock or 5% in one industry, which may mean that they own five competing firms, although there is a clear leader. The opposite is often true of hedge funds, they take too much risk, concentrating and leveraging with highly risky equities and strategies. The key to success lies somewhere in the middle.

Rebalancing

You may have heard that you can't go broke taking a profit. This is incorrect. Actually nobody ever becomes wealthy by taking profits. Taking profits diminishes compounding, which is what makes people rich. This is the main reason you will not get rich with mutual funds. They do something called rebalancing. When your holdings do well, the fund must sell off some of it to "reduce your risk" (reduce concentration) and when they do poorly they may buy more because it is "undervalued." Remember, Napoleon Hill, the key to success is maximizing focus and concentration, not minimizing it. He wrote his book based on 25 years of studying many of the most successful people and businesses in the U.S. He was writing in relation to knowledge and energy, but I have observed that his observations work financially as well. Warren Buffett says that "Diversification is for those who do not know what they are doing." I suggest it works well for beginners and after you learn you can begin to focus.

You can beat mutual funds and Warren Buffett even if you are not as good as they are at stock picking. Buffett because of the amount of money he has to invest and funds because of the rules placed upon them. Mutual Funds keep you from becoming rich. They will keep your money fairly safe and will grow your money in good times and lose it in bad times. They will not lose all of it at once but they will not provide a decent retirement either if that is all you invest in. One of the biggest problems with mutual funds is the lack of control fund managers and investors have because of laws and investment policy statements (internal rules). Investing your own money in your own way doesn't have to be risky or time consuming. One positive point that comes out of doing it yourself is that you stay informed of what is happening in the world, you acquire skills, and you may even accidentally stumble upon a great investment. It only takes one. Mutual funds will repeatedly sell a great investment in an attempt to rebalance your portfolio to "protect you" from not having enough diversification, as they constantly rebalance your asset allocation to match your risk tolerance and investment profile. Rebalancing is the biggest reason that you will never become rich.

The S&P 500 return does not report dividends, yet it can't be beaten by other funds. Some funds may do really well but determining beforehand which ones will succeed is much harder than identifying companies that will do well. The most important thing you need to know right now is that diversification will significantly slow down compounding and keep you from gaining real wealth from your investments.

Dollar Cost Averaging

The key to wise investing is to limit losses and maximize gains. This is not the same thing as reducing market risk, which is the objective of mutual funds. Successful investors limit losses and maximize returns. Mutual funds do not do either. They buy a bunch of stocks, some go up and some go down and they hold them all, but not forever. Buy and hold is the key, if you hold the right stocks, and keep holding them until you decide it is no longer a good investment. Mutual funds do not buy and hold in this sense because of rebalancing. They sell good investments that will continue to go up simply because they went up and buy more stocks that have went down and will continue to go down because they went down. No sane person would do this. This is based on the idea of dollar cost averaging (DCA). This means that when the price is lower you are buying more shares and when the price is higher you are buying fewer shares, so that your average cost per share is less than the average of prices paid. This is either a logical error or a marketing gimmick for two reasons. First, you want the price to increase, not break even but that is a smaller issue. The second and more important issue is that it doesn't matter. $100 is $100 regardless of the number of shares it buys.

DCA allows them to provide stable returns, small gains and losses, as opposed to large swings. This ensures you will never be truly wealthy or broke, and guarantees that you remain calm and keep handing them a check every week for the rest of your life. The argument goes like this: if you give us a steady weekly check, we'll invest at higher prices for fewer shares or invest at lower prices for more shares. This means that the average price is where you break even. This is technically correct but the amount of money invested is all that matters, not the number of shares. $100 invested is $100 invested regardless of how many shares it buys. If you have a required rate of return of 15%, then you need $115 back. Dollar cost averaging would say if you bought one share this month for $100 and 2 shares next month for $100 because the price fell to $50, your average cost is $200/3 shares = $66.67 and to get a 15% return you only need the price to be $76.67. Forget about the number of shares, it is an illusion to distract you from what is meaningful. The $100 still has to grow by 15% to give you a 15% return on the marginal amount or that specific $100.

Dollar cost averaging takes past returns into account and this allows positive returns to be reported more frequently. Notice that between the first and second month, you lost 50%. Dollar cost averaging allows that to be ignored and calculation starts over from the average level. This makes losses appear smaller and gains appear larger. You want your money to grow, not break even, right? You should never buy something *because* it is falling in price. I am not saying you should never buy something *that is* falling in price, just that you should have a good reason for buying it. I would rather lose money when trying to make it and learn from the mistake than learn nothing and keep doing the same thing.

Mutual Funds and Advisers

Mutual funds are not designed to make people wealthy; they are designed to reduce volatility. This does not mean they reduce risk, it means they reduce variability. True investors, both established and knowledgeable, must sometimes change course or make quick decisions in response to changing market trends; while mutual funds do neither. Stop losses and options (which I'll cover later) are far better than diversification for risk reduction. By the way, not one person that I am aware of who has ever held the number one spot, or even came close, on the Forbes 400 has been "properly" diversified. Buffett is diversified, (not "properly") but he didn't start out diversified. He is only diversified because of the amount of money he controls. He also says that only 6 of his companies are responsible for the majority of his wealth. He advises ordinary investors to invest like they can only buy 20 companies in their life time. What is he trying to accomplish with this advice? He wants us to think hard and long about what we invest in and take a long term perspective. This could be considered trend investing; it is just very long term trends. Buffet, in my view, is not a value investor in the traditional sense but a trend investor with a focus on value. He may not wait for the trend to begin but he is not looking for a trend in stock price. He is looking for a trend in society that has emerged or has shown signs that will emerge in the future. A huge investment in Burlington Northern is likely related to transportation or energy costs and the need to move goods at low prices. There may be more to it than that, but that is the general trend.

When mutual funds and financial advisers say reduce risk they mean market risk. They may also refer to it is as systemic or systematic risk. They ignore the other types of risk; such as business risk, political risk, economic risk, and currency risk. Financial advisors are also restricted in what they can and cannot say and many do not have much knowledge of investments, even if they think they do. Two rules for dealing with financial advisers if you choose to work with one - ask to see their degree so that you can see what it is in (you want it to be relevant to business) and know that the more confident the adviser seems the less he probably knows. There have been studies proving that as education increases, confidence decreases, as more data is being considered in decision making.

Financial advisers are salesman and they usually know more about how to get you to feel comfortable handing your money over to them than they do about how to grow it. They try to keep things simple, not so that you can understand it, but so you feel good about it. They do not want you to ask questions or be concerned. Their answers will almost always be to reassure you that everything is fine, rather than to educate you. In fact, I believe that as long as an adviser brings more clients and money in on a consistent basis, he could lose money for all the clients consistently and probably keep his job (as long as the clients do not lose faith and go elsewhere).

How can we start building wealth? Before I get into investments I want to say find what you love and put all your time and energy into becoming great. I have heard statistics that an education is by far the best investment a person can make, but you must gain relevant skills that are in demand and will continue to grow in demand (preferably in a field you love and are passionate about). You can find many examples of people who are known for one thing - Bruce Lee, Muhammad Ali, Mike Tyson, Michael Jordan, Warren Buffett, Bill Gates, Steve Jobs, etc. Now, you might say, "But I can't aspire to that level." Good news, you don't have to. Just trying to and focusing will make you better off than you would have been had you not tried.

Mutual Funds and Dollar Cost Averaging

Do not take profits off the table. Your investment is doing well. Why would you want to take profits to try to find another investment that is doing well? The logic is backwards here. People think that because the investment went up it is more likely to go down, but the reverse is true more often. If it is going up recently, it is more likely to keep going up than it is to go down. There are better methods for keeping your profits in your hands than selling great investments.

If a company were to grow by hundreds or thousands of percent, you should hold that company until you have a reason to sell it. Mutual funds have rules that they can never have more than a certain percentage of money in any one asset (stock) and one industry and they may have to hold a certain number of stocks in one industry at all times. So let's say they have to hold 5 banking stocks but they know one will perform better, they may only be able to invest 1% of total funds in that stock. This means that they must continually sell that stock (also triggering taxes) as it increases in value, reducing the percentage of money you have invested in it. They may also be forced to buy more of stocks that fall in value because they are doing poorly. What if banking stocks are known to be performing poorly and are getting worse? Mutual funds must still invest in the industry and try to pick the stocks that are less likely to plummet. Managing risk by knowingly investing in things that are going to do poorly is not wise. I would not even call that managing risk, I would call that stupid. I don't mean that the mutual fund managers are stupid, just that the laws regarding mutual funds are counterintuitive.

II. INVESTING LIKE A BUSINESS

How Businesses Diversify

Businesses, when they acquire other business or create joint ventures and alliances, do not seek to diversify into businesses totally different from their own. In most cases they seek to align resources and capabilities to reduce cost or leverage strength. When they do not do this, the venture often fails. Jack Welch, a well respected former CEO of GE, advises businesses to never carry losers. Businesses know through experience that this type of diversification does not work. So, why should we carry losers, especially on purpose? In fact, no business ever starts off as diversified and the only reason they do diversify later is not to reduce risk, but to create higher growth when growth has slowed. If you look around your city I will bet that the richest people are not diversified, they probably own one to two businesses or real estate and are heavily concentrated and knowledgeable about one industry. On a side note, companies that treat their customers well and have happy employees will perform better than those that do not.

CHAPTER 1: IDENTIFY POTENTIAL INVESTMENTS

Economics and History

Read as often as you can. Whether your goal is to become great at creating life saving drugs or an investment guru, reading will make a top-notch investor in biotech stocks or pharmaceutical companies. When you have superior information, you are better able to process that data compared to the average investor. History was always very boring to me, until I started to connect events to one another. It can be very interesting when you watch things unfold one step at a time and see how different people shaped debates around specific topics. Not everything in history is fun or exciting to read about, so pick topics that interest you. I started by studying recessions and depressions which eventually got me interested in presidents and how their policies either helped or hurt the economy.

I first started to learn about investments by reading about Warren Buffett. I was soon was reading every book on investments I could find, which included nearly every investment book in the library. I learned that the best financial goal shouldn't be getting out of debt once high rate loans are paid off; it should be gaining enough income or cash to cover it. I went on to read books about economics and especially recessions after 2008. I have found that the best way to learn is through experience and the recession was a great learning experience for me. I thought, this is a great time to buy, and I put my few measly dollars in banking stocks, only to lose it. I had loans taken out as well because of the "great opportunity" but fortunately I invested it elsewhere and my gains offset the losses. Not all falling companies are bargains and I learned to let a bottom form.

Huge trends create many investment opportunities and companies that grow from them, so do not worry about missing the boat. We always wait for a trend to begin, but we never wait for it to end. We also use common sense, which means we avoid following trends that do not make sense or are incomprehensible because they are short lived. We want to protect the wealth we already have above all else. Everyone saw the trend of smartphone demand, yet a clear winner was not as visible between Google, Apple, Nokia, Blackberry, Samsung, etc. These companies were already quite large as well, so growth would be slower than in a tiny supplier. Then I came across Qualcomm, which makes it possible for wireless devices to access the internet, its patented chips were bought by all of the big name companies. Qualcomm represented less risk, higher demand, a better market position, and more potential (markets outside of smartphones and supplier power with patents creating barriers to entry). Not to mention it had several quarters of earnings surprise after earnings surprise. These are the types of companies we are looking for: small companies with huge trends and strong market power. We are not only focused on return, but risk as well. We do not want the highest return possible. We want the highest return possible with the lowest risk possible. Note: Do not confuse small company stocks with penny stocks. Penny stocks are extremely high risk. Small companies can be extremely high risk as well but some are low risk, high return, stable, and obvious.

What about gold during recessions? Gold has done well but only because people thought it would do well and put their money where their mouth was. Does the value of gold go up because the government prints money? The answer is only if people continue to buy more gold. Demand pushes prices up, so if more money creates more demand for Gold the price will go up but not because the government printed money, it's because people bought more gold. Everything happens in cycles and there is nothing we can do to stop that. Here is what will happen if and when the economy recovers. Some other asset, stocks most likely, will begin to go up, investors regain confidence, and some will invest in stocks because they seem to offer more return now than gold. These investors will sell gold to raise the money they need to invest in stocks, putting downward price pressure on gold. As more people do this, stocks rise more and Gold falls more, because the money is moving away from Gold and to another asset. In the opposite scenario, in which the economy keeps getting worse, the unemployment rate is high and people want to eat. Who is going to buy gold from you and if they can afford it won't they take advantage of your hunger? If you believe that the government will allow gold to be traded as currency, doesn't it follow that they will be able to change and fix the price as well? The point is that with so much money moving into Gold already, sooner or later we run out of money that can be placed in Gold and therefore it can go no higher. Yet, when conditions create a good investment elsewhere, the money invested will likely be raised by selling Gold.

Top Down Approach

The top down approach starts by looking at the economy itself. Which country seems to have the most in its favor? You can determine this from the news and also from studying the companies themselves. Most developing countries do not have the same level of data or reliability of data as the U.S. but trends and patterns may emerge to help evaluate prospects. Next, the particular industries are examined for opportunities. Once an industry is determined to have good prospects, individual companies are singled out as leaders or as having good potential relative to risk. *Investor's Business Daily* (*IBD*) http://www.investors.com is a great resource to help with this. It is a daily newspaper that ranks industries and companies according to their fundamentals and technical reports. It will help you learn to read technical reports and spot small fast growing companies of high quality. If you read the *Wall Street Journal* http://www.wsj.com think about small companies that will benefit from large trends. *IBD* also focuses on a lot of small companies that you may not have heard of, but they will be much higher in quality than most tips you get in the mail about the "Next Big Thing". *Motley Fool* http://www.fool.com and *Seeking Alpha* http://www.seekingalpha.com are great websites to use in research. Louis Navellier's newsletters http://www.navelliergrowth.investorplace.com are also a great research tool; he has many options for different budgets. He not only helps you pick stocks and evaluate the economy and trends, but teaches you how he is doing so along the way. There are many monthly newsletters that cost about $50 per year and give advice. You may want to subscribe to many of these and evaluate the advice. DO NOT blindly take the advice, analyze it and watch to see what happens. The goal is to learn how traders think. You are only using these services to get ideas and learn. You should watch to see what strategies work and why. You may buy a stock for one reason and it may go up for a totally different reason. Real successful stock picking requires confidence in yourself and your decisions as the real money will take years to build and using many research tools allows you to develop your own system. If you read, research, and experiment, your "system" will come automatically. The one thing I want to emphasize is that while you can learn from other people's systems, you should never rely totally on someone else's system because that does not require you to think for yourself and if you do not think, you will not have good results. I recommend subscribing to *Value Line* as well as many financial magazines such as *Money*, *Smart Money*, *Fortune*, *Forbes*, and *The Economist* but to stay abreast of trends, and find ideas. I recommend that you skim the articles since you do not need to read the whole magazine. I usually read about new technologies and possible stocks that could benefit from trends but I do my own thinking and analysis. I will show you how to do your own as well.

What Industry to Invest In

What industries are growing? What industries are changing and full of uncertainty? What industries are being attacked in the media, by lawmakers, and the like? What Industries have high fixed costs and lots of debt? What industries rely on seller financing? When do these Industries do well and when do they struggle? These questions can keep you out of trouble. Take a look at *IBD*, which ranks industries by growth.

What industry do you work in? Should you invest in it? After Enron collapsed, there was a lot of overgeneralization and warning about investing in a company you work for because all of your eggs are in one basket and if you lose your job you could lose your savings at the same time. With that in mind, take note that if you just got a job in a particular industry, it may be because that industry is growing and demand is increasing. I am not saying that you should invest in the company you work for but putting some money in the industry might be smart. Just do not put all of your money there. Also NEVER invest all of your money; you should always have cash on hand. If stocks fall in value and all your money is invested, you lose money and you have no way of picking up deals. Having cash on hand gives you an advantage. Having cash on hand in a recession explains a significant part of Warren Buffett's wealth and strategy.

Right now, with income down, student loans high, and people still paying back mortgages from high prices homes (the future may see more people sharing a roof), and the economy still sputtering, many companies may struggle to keep earnings rising. The safest strategy is to look at companies with no or very low debt that do not rely on financing for sales; specifically, companies that sell low-cost items and necessities like utilities, food, energy, chewing gum, drinks, etc. Some competing products may be integrated with existing ones and become complementary instead of competitive. What companies are saving people time and money or making things easier? What companies have horrible customer service and do not seem to care about the customers' happiness, but only getting a contract signed and enforcing it in court without actually fulfilling their end of the deal? You may have to base answers on your own experiences. If you've had a bad customer experience, it's likely that others have too and you will see it show up in the company's financial performance at some point. It is likely that these companies are already struggling to make ends meet which could be the reason for the way they treat customers (more focus on paying bills than servicing customer).

Investor's Business Daily tracks the fastest growing industries for you and ranks them. It also keeps track of the fastest growing companies and charts them, teaching you how to trade technicals along the way. The strategy we will use is first to find an industry with good prospects. Next, we find a good company within those industries that is an industry leader who is doing much better than the industry and likely to continue to do so. If there is no clear leader, the next option is to invest in an ETF in that industry.

Penny Stocks

Penny stocks can double faster because it is easier to double 10 cents than 10 dollars right? Wrong. I will give you two reasons. First, the market capitalization of the whole company is what matters and the other is inflation of shares, like inflation of dollars, eroding the value of the shares. Second, market cap is what needs to double - the price per share multiplied by the number of shares outstanding. $100 million is $100 million no matter what the share price. Issuing new shares reduces the price and your percentage ownership of the company. Penny stocks or pink sheets are also not regulated. My personal rule is to rarely buy a stock below $10 and never below $5. I also look at market cap and prefer companies of $100 million to $10 billion for my "forever" holdings. There is a difference between small companies and low stock prices.

WalMart

Good companies and brands are not penny stocks. If you had bought shares of WalMart at its IPO in 1970 at $16.50 (the company was valued at $21.5 million) you would have actually paid one penny per share after accounting for its eleven stock splits, but it was never a penny stock. It also pays $1.92 dividends now. So holding onto the stock would be giving you a dividend so high in percentage it's tough to calculate. If you had bought one share at $16.50, it would now be 512 shares valued near $70 each and paying dividends of (512 x $1.92= $983 per year). If it paid one cent in dividends that is a 100 % dividend, so this is a 19,200% annual return from the dividend alone (if it's paying 2% based on today's price and you sell it to buy another stock paying 2% it's the same yield, it is your cost basis that allows it to be so high) so where and how can you get dividends like this. By finding strong companies and investing in them early and holding them forever. Even if you just invest $100 in a promising company you could be a millionaire if you hold on to it forever. If you get exposure to it in a mutual fund, they will continually sell it off. The one thing Buffett does differently than every investor - he never sells (a good business).

Some people are going to say, "But WalMart is one in a million. How am I supposed to find that one stock?" First, there are far less than a million investments, and far less than that are good ones. I am not saying that you should have seen WalMart and knew to place your life savings on it, but $50 would have been enough to be highly probable. You would have found it using the tools and strategies presented in this book. If you do not see stocks like that, you are not paying attention, especially with the help of *IBD*. If you think a company may be changing its industry, but you are not sure, just put $50 on it and wait, but never sell. Instead of putting the money in your mutual fund, find a different stock every week or month until you learn. This way you are focusing each investment and learning but overall you are diversified. Once you identify the best investments start consolidating the money.

Learn the difference between someone who is trying to educate you on how to pick stocks and someone who is trying to influence your decisions or push stocks. Make sure "buy" ratings are in relation to other investments. Many times they are in relation to their industry but not the entire universe of stocks. Keep in mind that a buy rating for a short term trader could be a very small gain with a reversal of opinion after that gain. You have to know what strategy the person making the call is implementing, which is why you should learn to invest for yourself. It is not hard, but only you know your time horizon and risk tolerance. It cannot be fully communicated because of emotions but you will learn to control emotions with experience. The best way to learn about investments is to do it, which is why I advocate using $50. First, you are already doing it (or should be) in your mutual fund or savings account so you will not miss the money. Second, you learn to control emotions and invest successfully with limited risk. So this is really another way to control risk.

We focus on one company at a time, while limiting our risk with stock selection criteria and also decrease overall risk by limiting how much money we place in each stock. So in the beginning, we may not be financially focused, we are just learning how to focus. It is a good idea to make your own list of attractive industries first and then look at buy ratings and how many analysts cover the stock. An increasing number of analysts covering the company, it is a good sign.

Business Strategy

Probably the most important aspect of a long term investment is its market position and potential. Michael Porter, a Harvard professor, has created what he calls the five forces. These are made up of buyer power, supplier power, the threat of new entrants, threat of substitutes, and the degree of rivalry. These forces are what Warren Buffett is evaluating when he says a company has a "competitive moat." Buffett wants his companies to have low competition, good potential, stable growth, and few threats.

Five Forces Explained

In my opinion, risk is best measured by Porter's five forces. Large buyers like WalMart have buyer power that restricts the profits of small suppliers. Because Proctor and Gamble has high supplier power, a strong brand and large company, WalMart does not enjoy the same price concessions as it does with tiny companies. Companies that create a new product with high returns attract competition so that profits are quickly eroded by competition. How do they offset this risk? High fixed costs can be one way, but a much better way may be patent protection. Can something else substitute for it? For instance, Monster energy drink is popular but you may decide to buy a different type of energy drink, soda or even water can be a substitute. The price of these other drinks places constraints on how much Monster can charge. The degree of rivalry is a measure of how competitive the industry is. If fixed costs are high, this means exit barriers are high, and competition may become so intense that no company makes a profit.

This is not as complicated as it appears. It is really just using common sense once you have an understanding of supply and demand and business basics. You want to invest in companies that have little competition, power over others, market leading positions that are growing, in industries that are growing. It is really that simple. Big money is made on companies that can change the world and defend themselves from competitors. That said there are many companies that have invented something, only to watch larger companies do it better and crush them. It is important to determine which companies have consistently adapted to new ways of doing things and stopped threats. They may be good investments and you may want to avoid small companies who are attempting to target them with competition. Small companies that are successful at taking business from large ones do it indirectly and slowly, flying under the radar. For example, it was not apparent that Amazon would be a major competitor to WalMart, until it was established and strong enough to respond to threats.

The Fundamentals

What to Buy

Fundamentals are the operations of the company. The numbers. We will look at ratios primarily. ROA and ROE will be equal if the company has no debt, which we like because no debt means less risk. ROA will be lower than ROE otherwise. There is no set hurdle rate for these because they vary by industry. Compare them to peers and see whose numbers are (higher) better. Sales should be increasing with earnings (operating earnings should be increasing). Earnings are often reported as EBITDA (earnings before interest, taxes, depreciation, and amortization) but do not use this measure if you have access to more accurate numbers. Cash flows are the most important measure of performance and operating earnings second. If sales are declining and earnings are rising, this could be a huge warning sign and we do not want companies with declining sales regardless of what else is happening. This does not mean we must sell the stock, but it does mean we have to get to work uncovering the reason or sell it. We do not sit by idly and watch while we are invested. We get involved or we get out.

Debt/equity - the lower the better. Many companies keep some debt to lower their weighted average cost of capital (WACC) because interest on loans is tax deductible. I like to see this ratio below 50%, but the type of business may require much higher debt. You want it to be lower than competitors, all else equal. If the debt is for massive research and development efforts to create new technology or lead an industry, the risk of the project and wisdom of the management are very important. Many great investments will pursue large scale projects to become leaders in new fields but they should not bet the company on one project if it can be avoided. You may want to lighten your holdings if you think it is represents too great a risk, but this depends on current market price. If it is at a 52 week low, you should have been out already. If it's at a 52 week high, momentum is on your side. Place a trailing stop on portion of the shares you own, not all of them unless you want out of the investment.

Isolate operating earnings from earnings and it should be growing. That is a must. Look at cash flows and make sure that inflows exceed outflows (unless it is a startup) and inflows are growing, especially operating cash flows. If outflows exceed inflows you need to know why and what the company is doing to grow inflows. How many years has the company paid a dividend and have they consistently raised it. For beginners, I would say if earnings are not increasing in a stable predictable manner and cash flows are negative, sell. You can still look into it to learn, but it's safer to do it from the sidelines. People often worry, yet stay invested, because they have been conditioned to do that by the buy and hold myth. Buy and hold works, but most people use it incorrectly.

If you invest for dividends reinvest them if you can but these companies should have long histories of steady and increasing dividends with the expectation of the same for the future and should be long term holdings. The dividends do not have to be reinvested in the same stock, but should be invested in the best opportunities. They also do not have to rush into an investment, it may be better to wait for better opportunities at times - but ALWAYS keep some cash on hand. Buffett could not pick up bargains if he were 100% invested because he would be losing money with everyone else. In a panic, cash itself becomes leverage.

The basic rule is to look for companies with increasing sales and earnings, an optimistic industry outlook, very a strong happy culture, and small enough to grow rapidly for a long time. Look for companies whose capabilities are superior to competitors, they are becoming a household name and have a recognized brand associated with quality. Let's look at a situational example of a company entering new markets and developing things that didn't used to be possible: drones that Amazon is creating to deliver packages. Is this only good news for Amazon? How about the parts suppliers who make those drones possible? How big are these companies and how much revenue is likely to come from this? This information will take some digging because most people do not think about this and these companies are probably too small to be mentioned on television. That creates an opportunity for savvy investors. Think outside the box about suppliers to large companies and research them. Find unknown companies. It is illegal to mention the name of tiny companies like these on television because of what it would do to the stock price, meaning few people know about them. They may be privately held but find out. The media will tell you what to invest in and about new technologies. You may do well taking their advice, but think about what they are not telling you that this could mean.

Keep in mind you have already determined the industries and trends to invest in. We are now looking for the cream of the crop. The best seller and most popular brand may not have the best numbers. This may be okay if they are addressing it and trying to fix it, not okay if they ignore or are unaware of it. A company that has better execution (better numbers) may still fail in that industry if the appeal of the product does not create rising demand, yet this company may have other industries in which it operates at the same efficiency rate and it is worth a look. You are coming to know the investments, the ones you invest in and the ones you do not. You need a comprehensive understanding of what you do not want to invest in, as well as why you are not and/or should not be invested in it. You will reject some investments of course but not before you learn about them.

Financial statements are very important for determining a company's ability to generate cash flows. Notice that I used the word cash flow, not earnings. Cash flows are harder to manipulate. Even when nothing unethical is done, earnings can vary by accounting methods quite dramatically and therefore aren't always reliable indicators. There are key ratios that will help you filter and narrow down your search for the best. The ratios should be judged against peers (competitors) in the industry, not against all stocks. Different industries have different dynamics that affect the ratios, such as the amount of debt needed or the amount of fixed capital (machinery) vs. variable inputs (labor, parts, etc.).

Fundamentals help you determine what to buy. Technical newsletters will help you determine when to buy (or sell). There are no set rules, but you may see someone advocate that you should not accept less than 12% ROE (return on Equity) or 8% ROA (Return on Assets). I think rules like this may help beginners but it also keeps people from thinking or developing their own system. And you will not become successful until you develop your own system. Why? Because you need confidence in order to control your emotions. This is one reason I advocate investing the money you are already investing in mutual funds into stocks, to build confidence slowly and with low dollar amounts. If you mess up in the beginning you are not losing much, and by the time you have created enough money to matter you have enough experience to make your own decisions without looking to outsiders. The key numbers you should be looking at follow.

Net cash flow should be positive, but doesn't have to be if outgoing cash flows are being used to grow incoming cash flows effectively. Growth companies may have negative net cash flow and either no earnings or high P/E ratio's. This is because fast growing companies generate earnings that are spent on generating growth (growing revenue - for example, building more stores) and this reduces earnings. In other words, they are generating more earnings than is apparent, which creates a high P/E and leads investors to conclude that it is overvalued. Most stocks that can ensure your retirement will be considered growth stocks and will likely have high P/E's. They will be considered too expensive by many and they may be for some investors, it is up to you to do your own analysis of future potential. All of these tools are helping you to come to a speculation about the stock's intrinsic value. It may look complicated and scientific but it is really just a guess and experience will help you get closer to intrinsic value. There are some complicated calculations you could do but it doesn't actually help you get any closer than a good guess; besides analysts have done this for you. You can find their estimates on any brokerage site. The consensus estimate should be used if you can find it. There are numerous ways to come to this but the easiest is just looking at the P/E. This is why it is so popular, it doesn't require thinking.

Technical Tools

Trends are spotted and capitalized upon by all successful people. Scientists build upon earlier scientific discoveries, where another scientist might have been "on to something." Investing is no different. Buffet looks for stable trends that can help predict the future operating performance of companies. Jesse Livermore looked for behavioral trends, although he would probably have called it price trends. He discovered support and resistance before we even had charts to track them. There are other types of trends like marketing trends, consumer trends, fashion trends, demographic trends, political trends, etc. This is what makes something predictable or foreseeable. People would like to get in on a trend at the very bottom and out at the very top, but this is much too risky. Not even Buffett claims that he can predict where markets are heading, although he recognized the bubble in 1987 and got out at the top, which allowed him to buy back at lower prices instead of sitting cashless and losing money with everyone else. So if we can't predict it or "time the market", we shouldn't try right! Well, good news, you don't have to time it to get out. Look at your potential "best buy" stock as determined by fundamentals and wait for a noticeable trend to appear. Find support and resistance on levels on the chart and place a stop loss just below support or, if there is no support because the stock is in an upward trend, you place a trailing stop to limit losses to a certain percentage. The more a stock has moved up though, the more it may correct, and the more room you may want to give it to fall so that you do not get out if you are a long term investor. This is up to you and your preferences regarding short term losses.

When to Buy

Fundamentals will help to determine what to buy but they can also be used to determine *when* to buy. If a company is having short term problems that are being blown out of proportion and it has a great long term strategic position, it may be a good idea to buy some of its stock. Don't put your life saving in it, since there could be trouble ahead. It doesn't matter how small the investment, whatever extra money you happen to have that could be used to purchase the stock will do; it will be a very long term holding. You are trying to make your money grow, it doesn't matter how small the investment is as long as you are growing your investment and learning. Having a long term focus gives you an advantage. The other traders have a different perspective since they may have owned the stock for years and do not want to lose their gains and have to wait years to recover them, or just have a quarterly goal to achieve.

Technical Signals

Technical signals will help us figure out when to buy after we have decided on what to buy. There are many signals, but they all do not have to be used. We will focus on the most important ones for our purposes; they are price support and resistance. They are the tools Jesse Livermore used and the only signals you need to know in the beginning to reduce risk. Basically if a price bounces up off of a price more than once that is support. It means buyers come in at that price and they are keeping the price from falling below that level. If price falls below that level, then the buyers have left the market and the price will likely keep falling. Resistance is just the opposite. It means that sellers are keeping the price from going above a certain price. If it pushes up through that price it is likely that it will keep going up. Support can become resistance once it is broken and resistance can become support. I would buy on a "breakout" - a push above resistance and place a stop loss a few cents below support. You will want to keep it far enough below that it does not trigger excessive trades, but close enough to get you out at a comfortable loss in the case of one. Moving averages can also be used in a similar way buying when the fast line crosses above the slow one and selling when it crosses below it. There are plenty of books on technical trading that you can get to help you with that. I am not an expert on the different types of technical tools and explaining them, but I do know that you can pick the tools you feel are useful. It has been my experience that many of the techniques do not seem to work, but it may be that I have not developed the skills for them. Some work well for me and it may just be that I like those better and understand them better. Most of these technical tools are for short term traders and day traders and while I like some of them, I am a long term investor and do not need to use the ones that do not align with my strategy.

<u>When to Sell</u>

Generally, if this were a new trade, we would sell when we would no longer buy. We have to forget sunk costs and only think about what is likely to happen in the future. If we need to sell something to raise cash, it is best to sell the weak performer or the investment with weak future potential based on fundamentals; which means those that are likely to decrease in price in the near term based on technical tools. If we do not need to sell for some external reason, or because we have found a better investment, our system will take care of getting us out at the right time automatically. There is a possibility that in extreme events a gap occurs in price, where selling is so strong that you cannot get out of the market. In this case you need to monitor your stocks and you may have to manually place a sell order. This is rare, and you likely wouldn't be able to get out of the market anyway in such a case, so our strategy is safer than not having it in place.

      The general rule is this: only sell if you have found a much better investment or the owned stock's future outlook has changed for the worse. I will say that the longer you hold the company the better, given that it has good potential. Until you learn how to determine that potential, use technical signals to keep you going until you learn more. This reduces risk. The riskiest thing you can do is put your money in something, do no research, worry and hope for the best and still do nothing (this is what your mutual funds and advisor encourage). The best thing to do in that case is sell the investment. Be careful selling an investment to buy another though. The new investment should offer a substantial increase in performance over the one held. If a really great investment comes along, you may decide to sell all holdings and invest totally in it, but be sure that the fundamentals (strategic and financial) and technicals (P/E, price) are good and then place a stop loss on it.

Strategy from Start to Finish

Find companies and industries with good potential based on Porter's five forces. Look for small companies benefiting from large trends in a market with low competition and high barriers to entry. These companies should already be well managed with little to no debt and easily beating analyst earnings estimates. Find technical support and resistance levels before buying and also determine an intrinsic value and do not pay more than this. (Intrinsic value is different for everybody depending on required rate of return and growth rate assumptions). Use cash flows and operating earnings to gauge accurate growth rates. Buy and place stop losses below support. Move the stop loss to a new support level if one is established. Keep repeating. The more companies you own the harder it will become to watch them all. Once you have built some money and confidence start consolidating by selling the investments you no longer see as the best opportunities.

CHAPTER 2: CONSIDER RISK AND RETURN IN CONTEXT

If someone offers to give you a tip about a stock that could soar 3,000%, you'd better believe the loss could be 100%, which is far more likely in most cases. Do your own research like a business would. If anything, limit the investment to very small amounts. This is what I advocate for beginners so you can learn to spot risky investments. I never buy anything on the pink sheets (OTC market). I have minimum and maximum market caps that interest me. I usually want to see stocks over $100 million and below $20 billion in market cap. I also want the stock price to be above $5. I prefer no debt, industry leadership, and huge potential, think wireless internet connectivity, drone technology, and driverless vehicles. I look for companies that make the end product possible without drawing much attention to themselves. They are not yet a household name, but may be in most homes. This means investors do not yet know about them either and mutual funds cannot buy them until they are larger. Also, rich investors could buy these companies if they find out about them but won't. Why? It's too small of an investment to matter much to the overall portfolio and it's illiquid.

Given the choice between a 10% return and a 20% return, I want the one that is more probable and a loss is less probable. Returns are predicted (forecasted) and cannot be known with certainty in advance, so focus on not losing money. Some industries are higher risk than others; you want high probability of making money and low probability of losing money. You will get better with experience and the strategy I have outlined is the least risky way to start investing on your own. Look for socially responsible companies that do not get attacked by consumers, the media, politicians, or their customers, suppliers, and media. You would rather they not get sued by competitors but if they do, make sure that you believe they can win the case (believe, not hope). Don't just study your investments, study their competition. What are the plans for the future? Are they doing anything radical or experimental? What could it mean to your investment?

CHAPTER 3: LIMIT THE DOWNSIDE

Risk and Return

The idea that to get higher returns you must take more risk is an inaccurate generalization. For mutual funds this may be true. Advisers will tell you that large companies are less risky than small companies. Again, they are talking about price stability vs. volatility. Remember, volatility can be good or bad and you can learn to mitigate the negative aspects. Buying stock in a risky company can be made less risky because of the investment strategy. Also, a small company is not more risky than a large company just because of its size. Advisers also only focus on marker risk, which there is little you can do about except diversify, according to them. There are things you can do and there are other types of risk can mitigate.

Types of Risk

Political Risk - Is it something the government may increase regulation on or discourage through higher taxes, like tobacco and alcohol? What about marijuana stocks and how the government influence sales.

Business Risk - The five forces is about competition and market position. It is desirable to be in a growing industry, in a company with the leading percentage of the market (more sales than competitors), and increasing that percentage of market. New markets are also desirable, as long as those new markets make strategic sense. For example, it could be unwise to create a market that has nothing to do with existing business and resources or capabilities. In other words, new markets should build upon strengths already present in the company and create synergies. You want your business investment to have rising earnings and sales. Rising earnings without rising sales is not sustainable. Don't forget that operating earnings are a more accurate assessment of sustainable earnings.

Economic Risk - This is a risk assessment of the economy as a whole. What are demographics like? Are most people near retirement age? If so, how will this affect businesses? There is always a bull market somewhere, as Jim Cramer says. If a trend in the economy is hurting overall economic growth, there will still always be some industry or company that benefits from this. If the population is aging, health care and pharmaceutical companies may be worth a look. What is the income, savings, debt levels of average citizens? In the U.S. we have had stagnating wages and rising debt for decades. Wages may now have to rise before company's sales can, but higher wages will put downward pressure on earnings. Focus on sales first, then earnings.

Currency Risk - Does the company operate overseas? This is becoming more common and this can lead to a situation in which the company and sales do well but earnings do not because of currency translation. The opposite can also happen. Many companies hedge this risk but some do not. Some companies hedge when they think it will adversely affect performance and they do not if they think conditions are favorable. The higher the percentage of business done in other countries, the more important this becomes.

Options

The first rule of options is always buy, never sell, until you gain more knowledge and confidence. One exception is if you have the cash to cover it and only then you can sell put options on an investment you already would like to own. This allows you to get paid to take the risk of the stock falling in value. In other words, if it falls below a certain price you MUST buy it. However, you are buying at a cheaper price than it was when you thought it was attractive and you got paid to buy it. If it goes up in price you do not have to buy it and you still got paid. The risk is that it may continue to fall after you have been forced to purchase it, so be sure that you will not have liquidity concerns or short term bill problems before doing this. Options prices are made up of intrinsic value, time value, and volatility. Intrinsic value is the difference between the market price and strike price. The strike price is the exercise price you pay for or the price at which you can buy (call) or sell (put). The longer the time left until expiration and the higher the volatility, then the higher the option price will be. Ideally you would want to buy long dated options in times of low volatility, just before a major move or large trend.

Buying Calls

Buying a call option is similar to buying a stock except cheaper. There is time value and volatility associated with the price. If you buy a call with a $20 strike, this means that you will have the right to buy it at $20. So if it's less than $20 you don't buy it and you lost what you paid for the call (let's say $2, but it is for 100 shares, so $200). You lost the entire investment $200. The same amount of money would have bought you 10 shares and if the price did nothing, you could sell and receive your $200 minus transaction costs. If you bought the stock and it fell to $19, you still only lost $10 ($1 per share). So why would you want to do this. Well let's assume the price goes to $30. You could have made $10 per share if you bought the stock at $20 and bought 10 shares, so you made $100 total and a 50% gain. Not bad. Ok, if you bought the call options for $2, or $200 for 100 shares, then you can sell 100 shares for $30 each, or $3,000 and simultaneously pay the $20 you agreed to pay ($2,000) for a profit of $1,000 using $200 of your own money. The profit just turned into $800 and the rate of return is now 400%. I only buy calls when I think there will be a big move in a short time, but I buy at the money calls with long durations.

Buying Puts

This is like shorting a stock. You make money when the stock falls in price. I rarely do this. I usually look for large moves over an extended period. Because there is a time element in the price of options; the longer you allow for a move to occur the more it costs. While downward moves can be big and fast, they are not usually stable trends, although obviously overpriced assets like gold, oil, and housing, may have a long way to fall once they begin to. If the market has recently been volatile the probability of a put paying off might be higher but volatility is also a component of price, so it costs more when markets are volatile. If you think the market will decline but it is stable right now, you would benefit both from the decline in price and the increase in volatility. The volatility is measured by the VIX Index.

Stop Loss, Technical Analysis

Stop Losses work by automatically setting a selling price at a predetermined price - which under my system would be based on support and resistance levels on technical charts. They can also work by setting percentage limits for falls in price. This is done when there is no support or resistance because we are in an uptrend which does not hesitate to establish these levels. The percentage you would set it at depends on your own assessment of the situation and your own strategy. The higher the potential and the more a stock is already up, the more room I allow for a correction but rarely would I allow a loss to exceed 20% unless I was already up much more than that. A stable growth company that is paying a dividend would also be given more room but not 20%. This also depends on the situation and company. This is why I encourage you to develop your own strategy. There will be times you break certain rules but you must know when to break them. These rules are to limit risk and learn. Once you can maneuver the markets and know how to analyze a company, your rules may change. At that point you will be more confident and know how to manage risk better; you will shift from protecting the money you have to growth mode. The companies that fall in value may become more attractive investments.

You started out by learning trader's tools to manage risk before you are confident in your abilities to find good investments. When you are confident that the company is a good long term investment, you may want to buy more when it falls. You may need to begin selling other investments that you deem to be less attractive, in order to start focusing your money in one great investment that is selling at better and better prices. The margin of safety (pay less than intrinsic value) should be higher for more volatile investments and it provides some risk reduction. Downtrends may continue for a while, allowing you to continue picking up bargains but you must have cash so don't get excited and go all in at once unless you are certain that it will soon reverse. You must also be sure that you do not invest money that you will need soon. This will make you too emotional regarding the money and this will lead to poor decisions.

Protective Puts

Some may advocate selling covered puts as insurance. Let me explain how this works. Let's assume you bought a stock at $20 and do not want to take a loss. You can buy a put with a strike of $20 and if it falls below $20 you can sell it for $20. The problem is that every time the options expire, you have to buy new ones. This strategy is often referred to as buying insurance against losses. I would rather take my chances with free stop losses. The only time that buying a put would be better is in an extreme event in which you could not sell your shares. We won't be selling any options as I mentioned and I can't think of any time I would want to sell a call, but selling naked puts (which can be dangerous if you don't have the money to cover it and the reason we don't do it) allows you to get paid to wait to buy a stock at a lower price. You must have cash on hand to purchase the shares at the agreed upon price or you can find yourself in trouble. You are guaranteeing the seller that if the price falls below a certain price; you will buy it, limiting their losses. They are paying you now to take this risk for them. A downside is that it may continue to fall for quite some time after you have purchased it.

III. DEVELOP YOUR OWN INVESTING STYLE

Chapter 1: What Not To Do

Do not try to copy Warren Buffett. Why? Isn't he much better than the rest of us? Well the answer has a few parts to it. First, he has a lot of money and there are two reasons why that matters. He cannot invest in tiny companies (he can but likely would not) because he would have to find multiple investments that all make sense. You see if he can invest $1 billion at 10%, which generates more cash flow than $500 million at 15%. What this means to you is that a company that may be a great investment, but has a market cap of less than $10 billion, for example, Buffett may not even consider, even if he thinks that investment is great. The second reason is because he is very liquid and has a long time horizon. His other investments pay him dividends, keeping him liquid at all times. He has time to wait for the trend to reverse. Just because he is buying does not mean that a recession has ended, he may be able to get deals the rest of us can't like preferred shares convertible to common with a 10% dividend. He also has incentive to spend money as well as save money. What do I mean by this? Well he is one of the richest people in the world and his wealth is tied up in the stock market. If the stock market goes down, his wealth does so as well, so he may invest and say wonderful things about the economy and America because his company depends upon it recovering and a recovery depends upon stable, rational people. Besides it is not good for anyone when everyone is in a panic and those with authority will try to calm the masses. Another reason not to copy Buffett or any other investor is because you need your own style that reflects your own personality and represents what you are comfortable with.

Some Successful investors who are obviously very different in investment style are Buffett himself (value investor), Jesse Livermore (technical trader or momentum trader), George Soros (currencies and bonds), and Carl Icahn (corporate raider). I do not think that any of these guys could copy the other and do well. They all did it differently and they were all successful. Jesse Livermore made a fortune in the recession of 1929 betting that markets would decline. An important nugget of wisdom here is that markets move faster on the way down than on the way up. Word of caution, never short a stock, buy a put option instead. Shorts have unlimited risk and limited potential (100% max if the company goes bankrupt). Puts are less risky and offer higher upside for smaller moves.

Do not buy or sell because an expert said to. Some are entertainers and may have their own reasons for putting a buy or sell stamps on stocks but talk about so many that you will get confused, hyped up, and excited. There are far too many ideas and potential concerns on the television channels about stocks. It is a good way to stay current on news but they encourage far too much trading and if you watch these programs you will be tempted to get in and out and back in again, always searching for higher yield. Financial news is geared toward very short term trading and if you can keep that in mind, it may be a good place to learn the language and get accustomed to certain aspects of the market. It should at least get you excited about investing.

The news gets you focused on short term results. I am going to teach you how to look for long term winners, that make money right now, quarter after quarter, without even having to watch the news.

CHAPTER 2: GETTING A STRATEGY

Investments Strategy

Companies may have good or bad strategies but you must also have a good investment strategy. Buying good companies with bad strategies may leave you worse off. I do not recommend trying to copy others. Their strategy may not work for you. Your strategy has to be understandable to you and also has to suit your personality. Few, if any extremely successful investors have used the same strategy. You may see books telling you that "all you have to do is" buy low P/E stocks buy; momentum stocks; buy stocks at 52 week lows; or 52 week highs. Some readers may read the book that says buy at 52 week lows and read another that says buy at 52 week highs and determine that either nobody knows for sure how to invest or investing is too confusing to understand. The reality is that these are two different strategies that both may be successful with certain types of companies at specific times. It is not likely that both strategies could work at the same time. You need to develop your own strategy.

Developing Your Own Strategy

I propose you stop putting your money into mutual funds and use that money to experiment with stock investing. This limits your risk because you are starting with small amounts of money. You will not miss the money because you are already contributing it. In the beginning, each time you buy a stock, pick one using a particular strategy with the goal of learning how to use that strategy. The goal should also be to not lose money. The goal is not to make money at this point, although that would be nice, it is far more important to learn. You may not want to do this if it means losing an employer match. Don't worry, you can invest extra money. But also know that gaining knowledge will likely be more profitable and possibly far more profitable than that match. Also know that while the first rule is to never lose money, this is a goal, not reality. Money will always be lost at times, whether you are in mutual funds or stocks, and the only thing you can do about it is limit losses. Mutual funds do not allow this, but ETF's do. So if you like the safety of diversification but want to limit losses, ETF's may be the perfect solution. This is because they trade like stocks, so you can place stop losses and protective puts on them.

You may have more than one strategy you rely on. You may have some value stocks and dividend stocks that are long term and buy when they decline in price. You do not want to sell these long term holdings, so there is no risk reduction strategies like stop losses. Your margin of safety is your risk reduction technique. You may have growth stocks and momentum stocks that are more short term in nature and have stop losses. Ideally, you will be looking for growth stocks that are expected to grow for decades but be aware that the industry could change with competition and new technology.

Building Confidence

Start small with many trades that are each $100 or less until you have gotten a style developed for yourself. You will need to research many ideas and competing theories and try them out for yourself. Some strategies do not work at all. Some work, but only for some people, as some take more time, patience, dedication, or whatever it may be. What works for one will not work for others. If a strategy does not work for you, it may just not be the right style of investing for you.

The one thing to remember is that you WILL lose money when investing no matter what you do, whether you are diversified or not, whether you are good at it or not. The more diversified you are the higher the likelihood that some of your investments are losing money. Mutual funds prevent you from learning how to become a better investor. You have to fail at things before you get good at them, even the simplest things. You could not walk until you crawled, stood, fell many times, and took one wobbly step after another, but you kept trying and you kept getting better. Failure is not to be ashamed of. Mistakes make us who we will become. I am not sure who said it, but my favorite quote is "The difference between losers and winners is that losers do not fail enough." I made this my life's guiding principle and decided that to become an expert I have to try, whether I lose money or make money, and take notes in order to learn. I had to spend a lot of time and money to attain the level of understanding I now have. The beauty is that I get to pass it on and hopefully save people years of research or change a direction that they take and make them better off financially. The key to learning is doing and the key to continuous learning without bankrupting yourself is to focus on individual investments and keep each investment low enough so that it would not bother you to lose it all but high enough so that you can at least make back the transaction costs. The goal in this process is to learn and not lose money, not to get rich. That will come later. It cannot possibly come before confidence; your emotions will not allow it.

It is much easier to evaluate a company than it is to evaluate a fund. I am not even sure a fund can be accurately evaluated for future performance. There are many ways of evaluating them, but they are all based on past performance, not future outlooks. I do know for a fact that a company can be evaluated and it is easy. It can be time consuming but doesn't have to be. It can just be looking at the SWOT analysis and five forces, fundamentals, and technicals. Technical analysis can be done in seconds or minutes once you learn to do it. Fundamental analysis can also be done fairly quickly. The SWOT and five forces can be thought about while doing other things throughout the day.

Once you have gained experience and knowledge, your goal should be to find five industries or trends that you think will do well for a very long time and then find companies that you believe will lead the industry and invest heavily in those, while using stop losses and monitoring technicals closely. If you cannot identify which companies will lead, then find an ETF for the industry as a whole until a clear leader emerges. The benefit to ETF's is that they trade like stocks, meaning you can place stop losses on them. This is a huge advantage over mutual funds. Oh, and they don't tie your money up for decades and try to lock you into paying them every week before you yourself get paid, another huge advantage.

CHAPTER 3: START FOCUSING

Once you have gained confidence and feel like you know what you are doing, start consolidating your investments. Start by getting rid of anything you are unsure about, that is showing weakness or declines in fundamentals or technicals, or just makes you nervous. Anything that has lost money has value in tax write-offs up to $3,000 per year. Anything over that must be carried forward to the next year. You want to try to get down to five stocks. These are your best ideas, one for five different industries. In some industries like technology, there could be multiple good investments so if you can't choose set a limit (1/5 of the portfolio) for that industry. When comparing two great investments, it may be necessary to do your own calculations and this can be done with a BAII plus calculator or excel. I will demonstrate how this is done, but at this point we are going beyond the scope of this book and getting into details that may distract you. The most important thing is that the numbers are increasing, the debt is decreasing or zero, and the strategy offers large potential with low risk. Most of this can be seen through the numbers but does not require modeling. The simpler something is, the more reliable it will likely be.

BAII Plus

Buy a BAII plus financial calculator and learn how to use it. You don't need to do this but it helps you understand compounding and it can be fun to play with numbers and see what happens. You can also use excel but we will focus on the BAII plus and the five most commonly used buttons on it. N is the number of periods. I/Y is the interest rate per period. PV is the present value (the amount you have to invest today), PMT is the amount of the payments you will make, and FV is the future value. If you know at least three of these you can solve for one of the others and you need to remember to use negative signs for cash outflows (the money you invest).

Now let's use an example of a $85,000 mortgage and a payment of $417 (6000 annually) at an interest rate of 4.75%. We want to know how many years it will take to pay this mortgage off. We put 4.75 in for I/Y, 85,000 for PV, -6000 for PMT, and 0 for FV, and hit CPT N to get 24.08 years. Let us now say that I have an extra $400 per month that I could invest or pay on the mortgage. Just change the PMT input to 10,800 (6,000 + 4,800) and hit CPT N to get 10.09 years. So we get out of debt 14 years faster. Now I have 14 years longer to retirement that I can invest. Now I am going to put the entire amount that I was paying on the mortgage into investments. Let's say that I invest $1,000 per month at 12% per year for 30 years. Starting with no money I end up with nearly 2.9 million dollars. So this takes 40.09 years because it took 10.09 to pay the house off. Now let's assume that I pay the minimum mortgage payment and invest $400 for 24.08 years with the same success (everything else the same). N=24.08, I/Y=12, PV=0, PMT=4800, CPT N= 572,674. I am not done. There is still 40-24.08=15.92 years to go. So I have N=15.92, I/Y=12, PV=572,674, PMT=1,000, CPT FV = over 3.5 million dollars. So I made $600,000 more not paying the home off early. The higher the return, the bigger the difference gets and 12% is average. This kind of calculation can come in handy. To compare two investments you would put PV = current stock price, FV= expected future stock price using analyst estimates or your own target, PMT= can be 0 if you aren't going to buy any more or 50 if you will purchase $50 per period and if dividends are paid they can be entered as a negative number, I/Y will either be solved for or plugged in as your required return, N= the number of periods.

It is not necessary to do all these calculations in order to be successful, but it is one more tool you can learn to use. You will find that there are many tools to use and different people and companies will teach different ones. You do not need to know how to use them all, just find what works for you and use common sense. If you don't understand something do not try to use it and if you can't figure something out move on to something else and forget about it. Don't let one tool frustrate you and keep you from success. Remember, you are going to succeed.

www.ingramcontent.com/pod-product-compliance
Lightning Source LLC
Chambersburg PA
CBHW031517210526
45464CB00007B/2956